On Loving a Saudi Girl

On Loving a Saudi Girl

Carina Yun

HEADMISTRESS PRESS

Copyright © 2015 by Carina Yun.
All rights reserved.

ISBN-13: 978-0692536902
ISBN-10: 0692536906

This book may not be reproduced, in whole or in part, including illustrations, in any form (beyond that permitted by Sections 107 and 108 of the U.S. Copyright Law and except by reviewers for the public press), without written permission from the publishers.

Cover art © 2015 by Carina Yun.
Cover & book design by Mary Meriam.

PUBLISHER
Headmistress Press
60 Shipview Lane
Sequim, WA 98382
Telephone: 917-428-8312
Email: headmistresspress@gmail.com
Website: headmistresspress.blogspot.com

for my mother and father

My candle burns at both ends;
it will not last the night;
but ah, my foes, and oh, my friends –
it gives a lovely light!

--Edna St. Vincent Millay

Contents

Sea of Marmara	1
Istanbul	2
Daughter's Letter Home	3
The Siren of Princes Island	4
Sunken Cistern	5
Sentimental Education	7
Festival of the Sacrifice	9
Reading Edna St. Vincent Millay	10
Lost Her	11
Cover	12
Meditations After Stein	13
Salvage	14
The Lamppost Watcher from the Window	15
On the Anniversary of Your Disappearance	16
In Therapy I Painted a Piñata Doll	17
Hysteria on Melancholy Street	18
Ten-hour Notebook	19
On Loving a Saudi Girl	21
The Green Umbrella	22
Through the Stockton Street Tunnel	23
Powell Street	24
As He Lay Dying	26
The Day After My Father Died I Speak to God	27
Mortuary Band On Stockton Street	28
Poem I Wrote for My Father to Say to Me	29
Girlhood	30
Prayers	31
Letter to Emily Dickinson	32
Acknowledgments	35
About the Author	37

Sea of Marmara

There is stillness behind her
Each crescent empties my body

As I lie on the broiled sand
Her hair stolen from a falcon's nest

Eyes borrowed from fig vines
Lips plucked from dry rose petals

Her curves now a wild spirit
As she whispers, Millay

Love has gone and left me

*

Love has gone and left me
Nights, I drift to where the waves

Rush the shore
To a woman kneeling in saline water

Her wrinkled mouth slippery
Above the sea's surface

Her eyes a shadow, audacious
Against the pillars of Sultan Ahmed

Often, I wake with violent sweat
My legs tangled in her seaweeds

Istanbul

A ten-year-old boy asks me
        to buy a fake gold watch.

I look at handwoven
        pashmina scarves strung by the door.

Two hundred lighted glass lanterns
        dangle from the ceiling dome.

A soumak rug is unrolled on the floor,
        dust rising in the air.

Six apple tea glasses,
        a white sugar cube dissolves.

In front of the marble bathhouses,
        I tug my headscarf tighter.

The pillars of Hagia Sophia glow in the dark,
        Judas leaves fall to the ground.

A man selling pink roses wants
        to take me on a Bosphorus ride.

I take the 8 p.m. ferry, fall asleep
        and wake by sunrise.

Love songs enter the bosom, *muezzin*
        sings lullabies over the Blue Mosque.

Ten missed calls: *Li Li,*
        it's your father, please come home.

I study the Turkish paper,
        feet warming under the blankets.

Daughter's Letter Home

Dearest Mother,

It is the beginning of morning twilight in Istanbul.
The sun arrived early,

Drawing a bright orange line above the Blue Mosque.
Soothing morning prayers over a microphone woke me;

It lifted my spirit and sang me a love song,
Allahu Akbar, Allahu Akbar.

In that instant, my body filled with warmth.

But the frosty Black Sea air has a way of seeping
In through the louvered windows.

Mother—women cover their faces here.
Yesterday evening, when I took the ferry over to Asia,

I met her.

She was encased like a Matryoshka doll—
The color of soot, but her irises warmed deeply into mine.

I was certain she smiled at me from behind the veil.
I wanted to let out my creaky voice,

But instead, I stared at the stodgy man sitting beside her.

Mother, what is life if I have to hide behind a veil?
What is life if I am wrong to love?

The brittle Black Sea is more than I can bear.

The warm breaths have left like smoke—
Muezzin has sung his last verse.

The Siren of Princes Island

Dusk by the Marmara Sea
Her eyes painted blue-green
She relinquishes her umber hair
And shows me her elbows and knees

She bribes me with a secret
Guides me to a buried room
Filled with treasures: a boy's boot
Behind a grandmother's sweeping broom

Dusk by the Marmara Sea
A carriage crosses the island
Two white stallions gallop
Their hooves polished like diamonds

Bewitched by her siren song
I tiptoe into her marble room
Where I discover her ring
Tied to a baby's spoon

Dusk by the Marmara Sea
She kisses my hair
Then reaches for my silver and buttons
My only purse now bare

Sunken Cistern

West of the Hagia Sophia,
five hundred feet underneath the foxhole,
Medusa's headstone fractures in the canal.

*

Across the Roman columns,
the auburn candlelight blushes as
a mistress undresses and lies in my bathtub.

*

She bends her elbows and knees.
Her viridian irises close.
My mouth fills with damp sand.

*

Morning devotions inside the Blue Mosque,
I cleanse my filthy hands
then kneel—head on the marble floor.

*

On the Bosphorus ferry,
I fall asleep and dream of the Sea Witch.
Her legs made of Persian seaweed.

*

On Princes Island,
I ride a 19th century phaeton across
the Judas leaves with two white stallions.

*

My stiff body descends into water,
knots in my breasts,
seaweed tangled around my waist.

*

Inside the sunken cistern,
Medusa's eyes open.
My ventricles turn to stone.

Sentimental Education

She slips off her wedding band and places it on the Prussian blue granite

Here in the classroom, Professor Goyce hands me a Turkish dictionary

I write compositions on Constantinople

The city was originally founded as a Greek colony

I look for three words

There in the stone bathhouse, she unbuttons

I quickly hide my filthy hands

Arin… we shouldn't

under the name of Byzantium in the 7th century BC

Her mouth on mine, my body pushed against the wall

Constantinople was the largest and richest urban center

Professor Goyce walks by my desk

I look down at the words smeared on my hands

in the Eastern Mediterranean Sea

She looks into my dilated eyes, her chalked hands pressed
        on my tablet armchair

Constantinople was famed for its massive defenses

Her right hand slides up

Arin…

the city, and the Empire, would ultimately fall to the Ottomans

There, I scrub the filthy words off my hands

There, I pick up her wedding ring

Festival of the Sacrifice

Dearest Love, the Grand Bazaar has closed
for the week. Goats are sliced and left bleeding
on the street. I pass between them with my black
leather boots as the sun pulses down on plots
of Bermuda grass. The days go by slowly.
Sundays, I take your book and read by the tram
station. People stare at their phones.
The tram suddenly stops in front of me, as if
you were announcing "I'm here…"
and always the doors slide shut in front of me.
I'd watch two adolescents kiss while the tram
wisps away. Last night, you appeared in my dreams.
You said, *those that really love, love in silence,
with deeds and not with words,* and placed
a buttercup daisy on my tablet armchair.

Reading Edna St. Vincent Millay

I think about the morning's *muezzin*
waking me at four-forty, his song
solemn, I'd stumble out of bed

and bend my knees on the soumak
rug not knowing whether to repent
for those mornings spent under

the fragrance of her umber hair,
the Turkish paper sprawled over us
as she read, or the mornings waking

to the smell of thick coffee,
poured into a ceramic mug painted
with her celadon eyes; it seems

her eyes follow me on deserted walks
over the Galata Bridge, the fisherman's
line pulling beside the fence, a trapped fish,

I wouldn't ever know why she threw
her pearls into the sea, I should have
forgotten her already, but her eyes,

I miss them, her breath I miss,
how to think of those days, as now,
when Millay describes the knots

that bound her beneath the earth's
soil, and the sounds of renewed rainfall
beating on the thatched roof.

Lost Her

to a Turkish boy's marriage proposal.
Lost her to cleansing my hands and feet behind the Blue Mosque.
Lost her to morning *adhan.*
Lost her to where I laid my head on the marble floor asking God
    to forgive me.
Lost her to her secret kisses in the stone bathhouses.
Lost her to copperware, amber prayer beads, water pipes,
    grandfather coins and candlesticks.
Lost her to walks over the Galata Bridge, facing the grieving
    Black Sea.
Lost her to ferry rides over the Bosphorus.
Lost her to pomegranate juice, roasted chestnuts, and kebab
    sandwiches.
Lost her to cinnamon bark, dried rosebuds, Indian saffron, and
    crushed red pepper.
Lost her to stray cats and pups sleeping by the laundromats.
Lost her to *Eid-ul-Adha,* goats sliced and bleeding on the street.

Cover

salt
soil   veil
wave
cover   the head
hair
lip   compress
wind
cover   the sea
mouth
robe   dress
modest
cover   wound
news
box   brandy
body
cover   the sin
father
woman   kiss
cover
covering   the covered

Meditations After Stein

A life
Her and I her and I
Without name or glory
Without I without name
God and I God being I
God knows I am this way
Come to terms with terms with
God and I
Her and I
The way the right way

Salvage

What I dreamt. (one) Remains swept into the dust pan:
hair strands, sweet honey crumbs and mix
molded grains. (two) A cold breeze from the foyer
to the kitchen stove, the memory of her
in peculiar spaces. (three) The slow burn
of a teakettle whistling from the stovetop.
Put down the poems and make the tea, it said.
(Four) I drive for two hours and forty-one
minutes. I watch the mortician peel back
the white sheet. It feels like four degrees.
The mortician catches me when I collapse.
I want to crawl on top of her corpse and die.
Time: seven hours ago. (five) What's not used:
ballet flats and her cardigan. I did not come
to the realization yet. I wake crying,
my airways tied. (six) In a dream, she brings
a coffin back from the dead, a trail of sawdust
on the floorboards. She lifts the coffin lid
and says, *lay in it with me.* (seven) I didn't
dare make a sound. The lining is velvet. (eight)
Don't leave me, she says. (nine) I forget to breathe.
(ten) I could no longer see.

The Lamppost Watcher from the Window

a mix
        precipitation
        wintery lamppost
        slow sullen drops
        by mid-afternoon
light rain
        hair on window glass
        one royal flicker
        cloudy and gusty
        temperature near
exhale
        warm condensation
        you accumulate
        muffles musty words
        finger circles glass
oval forms
        you leap to coat
        hung hanger raincoat
        thick padded bootstraps
        feet on cement
violent
        wind combs black silent
        your hand on broken glass
        but you flinch back
        flat into lamppost
speak
        (silence) drags your feet
        absent
        her cheek on your cry
        a little silent
knife

On the Anniversary of Your Disappearance

I dreamt I saw you in a field of ocher
You plucked sunflowers
By their hairy stems and peeled back

The coarse-toothed leaves
You were a child, maybe three
You didn't pull back when

The bee huddled by the florets buzzed
You parted your tiny mouth
And stuck out your tongue

And the bee flew right in
It was silent then
You pursed your lips and spat out

A dead bee—its colorless wing torn
You said it hurt
You hurt

I was that bee

In Therapy I Painted a Piñata Doll

gave her a navy blue face
with scarlet cheeks.
She wore a birthday fedora,
polka dot blouse, rainbow socks,
pink lipstick with a frown.
Her left arm having been severed
by a gigantic mahlstick—
her insides pouring, sweets suspended:
Christmas candy cane,
                movie stub,
Pink Pearl eraser,
                Dixon Ticonderoga,
Queen of Hearts,
                Webster's Dictionary,
razor blade,
        bottle of prescription pills,
bloody bandage,
        thirty one scattered unlit
                      birthday candles,
used tampon,
        dice, yellow crayon,
a box of matches,
                goose feathers,
hair ribbon,
        a golden penny.
Her left arm rests on the carpet floor.
Her fourth finger is missing from the canvas.
She points to a kerosene lamp—
the fire still lit.

Hysteria on Melancholy Street

My love stood in the middle
of the street with a black umbrella

water pouring out of her mouth
through her glossy lips

down her torso
into the sewage hole behind her.

Street signs swung counter
clockwise and dark colored sky.

My body startled by
the speeding cars and lamplights.

She couldn't hear my crying
out for her.

I wanted to run into the street
and stick my hand into the roof

of her mouth like a socket plug.
I wanted to tell her to stop it

but I couldn't open my mouth
because it was stapled shut.

The water, now a river
bleeding into the shadows.

Ten-hour Notebook

terminal two   Siamese cries
inside   rolling suitcase

a woman slides the back of her hands
around my breasts taps my ankles

do not   do not forget
the mermaid coins

boarding pass   under black skin seat
24: Afraid? Of whom am I afraid?

running eyeliner
have you been crying?
                      what if I were seen

*

baby diapers   spotted in back row
116: I measure every grief I meet

grandmother knits long slender scarf
and asks *Emily Dickinson?*

yes
what does she see?

100: Who is it seeks my pillow nights?

turbulence
(lady's broomstick hidden behind front curtains)

*

(unbuckle)
the wiping of orange juice stains

that witch points and says   *buckle*
36: She died at play

roll (my eyes)
light switch and lean watercolors

139: A long, long sleep, a famous sleep
ten nine eight hours time

I dream she's alive in white cotton
kisses me

and sweeps me up
with many-colored brooms *still*

*

wake *still*   alive *still*
alone *still*   vain *still*

my posture not right *still*
can't breathe *still*

my mother's ten missed calls *still*
only the swift sounds of winded rain *still*

I don't know how to tell you
I love you   *still*

you're gone   *still*
still

On Loving a Saudi Girl

After your beloved leaves, you will take
a ten-hour red-eye flight back to America.
At baggage claim, you will wait for your bag
to drop onto the conveyer belt, then drag
the weight of Sultan Ahmed across the terminal—
the soumak rug, candlesticks, and pashmina scarves.
In Istanbul, *muezzin* will call out five
times a day from the minaret. It's heard
on loudspeaker in every house, and every storefront.
You will wake to morning *adhan,* not knowing
whether to repent for those moments spent with her.
What is it called when you are wrong to love?
In front of the airport, your mother will find you
soaked with rain. "What happened?" she will ask.
You won't speak. She will spring open your
father's green umbrella and hover.

The Green Umbrella

> *"Like rain it sounded till curved—"*
> *—Emily Dickinson*

I watch the earth darken
      foreboding as if tell-
           ing, twirl the umbrella

greedily and warble
      as a bird. Meanwhile, my
           father shouts, he slams shut

the front door. I slip on
      the asphalt and watch my
           first love tumble over

like a bucket collect-
      ing for the first drought, be-
           low a wheel of black clouds.

Through the Stockton Street Tunnel

a butcher hangs the neck
of a Peking duck,

while two women yell prices
of dried shriveled squid and tofu skin.

Next door, big tins of Skyflake crackers
are being stacked to the ceiling.

Two weeks the city pours
and I am drenched like the sliced catfish

lined up on the street. I carry my mother's
wet bag of pig liver and chicken feet,

watch an old man spill withered
bean sprouts,

watch a grandma rope her grandchild
onto her curved back, and

then pick from the street. Meanwhile,
I tiptoe on the spilled fish water.

I tiptoe, following my mother to the
poultry house, listening to

her bickering through the tunnel.

Powell Street

A homeless man begs
with a filthy Styrofoam cup.

A union strikes outside
Macy's with cardboard signs.

A toothless woman grabs
my wrist. She asks me for my

baby teeth. It is pouring ice
pellets in July. My mother

clutches my tiny hands
and skids down the street

pulling me. My hair dries
under her open coat.

An old man in a hospital
gown pushes a wheelchair

to the food bank, cigarette
butt hanging from the corner

of his mouth. He carts
five bags of stale bread,

while I stand in the meal line
with my mother, smelling

the stench of urine and thinking
of all-you-can-eat buffet.

In the soup kitchen, a girl
with disheveled hair

drops her brownie. Her
cries like a calf being weaned

from its mother.
I give her my brownie,

each bite as precious as
jade through shop windows.

As He Lay Dying

under the azure ceiling,
            cracked with chipped paint,
I wonder how would I remember
            him ten years from now?
In a week he will have died
            his legs now heavy bricks.
At sunrise, I watch my mother
            drip tears into a bowl of oatmeal
as she feeds him with a silver spoon
            and wipes the corners of his mouth.
He sleeps alone in a chilly room,
            still inhaling and exhaling,
every breath carrying him
            to a different world—
a world I do not know.
            I enter his room with salt
dripping down my cheeks
            like the chipped paint on the ceiling.
He sees my eyes with their
            cracked red veins, dry.
I have no more tears, I said.
            My father says—*It's okay, Li Li.*
He unfolds his gaunt hands for me.
            I cover both his weathered hands,
the bruised memories
            hidden from view.

The Day After My Father Died I Speak to God

In the first hours of the morning
                                      when the sun has not risen yet
I sit up in bed
       still seeing his bruised body
I sit up in bed
       wondering if he heard the men zip up the body bag

In the dark, I ask Him—
                    where and as if He answered
a faint ray of sunlight sweeps
                           through the blinds

Mortuary Band On Stockton Street

The trumpet men play his name
as they ride through the streets.
They shout high from their horns
and croon from their chests.

We stare from the sidewalk,
stare into a widow's eyes as she
straightens her face, stare at his
picture as they parade.

We file like ants on the sidewalk,
our backs pressed against boxes
of dried fish and cabbage, our umbrellas
anchored carrying the weight.

We watch for the hand in the hearse
throwing spirit money into the rain.

Poem I Wrote for My Father to Say to Me

When I am gone, my dearest,
weep no tears at my feet;

Need not lay tender chicken breasts
nor tangerines on my lawn;

Need not tame the Zoysia
but let it decorate with its vivid green;

Let your mother burn spirit money
into the black pit, smoke rising

from the Eastern shore;
Listen to the monk's bells,

let them echo and lift your chest;
Write my pretty song—

let them fertilize and climb my home,
sing every word to the mountainside.

Girlhood

In the basement,
                my mother's broken washing machine spits.
Behind the staircase,
              he has my birthday present—
     his old Brandy box,
          a pack of Marlboro cigarettes, and Santa's red hat.
My father says I should have been a boy.
                I wiggle the front
                      of my teeth and make a wish.
        I want to be a boy.
He carries a cardboard box
              of things I do not need.

Prayers

Answer me when I call, Lord.

    My father's voice pulsates
which feels like an earthquake, he pumps
his hands and my mother chokes

    The first time I hear my mother cry
I squeeze my rubber duck until the water
drips out

    My father wraps his fingers
around my mother's neck like he's trying
to slaughter a duck

    My mother's belly is a watermelon
my sister is going to squirt out of her
like a black seed

    A fury rises inside me, Lord. I rip out
a clothes hanger and swing wildly
throw my whole body onto him

    I cry for you, Lord, blood glazing
down my forehead, a hook sliding
across my ribcage

    My father surrenders his hands,
but I have not yet lost the tremors, Lord,
and the scar across my chest

Letter to Emily Dickinson

I swing my father's arm,
      the morning air moisten-
            ing my long jet-black hair.
I pull out my letter
      tucked inside my orange
            peacoat and rashly drop
my father's hand, hover
      over the sweaty mail-
            box, press my lips, sway my
heels, pull back the wet damp
      lever, pull hard, and slip
            in my kiss. And this is
what I want to remem-
      ber: the lever swinging
            back, a thump, and the reach-
ing for my father's hand,
      the city fog cover-
            ing the better of us.

Acknowledgments

Gratitude to the editors and staff of the following journals where these poems first appeared:

Adrienne: "On Loving a Saudi Girl," "Sunken Cistern," "Sea of Marmara"

Calliope: "Daughter's Letter Home," "As He Lay Dying"

CutBank: "Reading Edna St. Vincent Millay"

The Feminist Wire: "Girlhood"

The Northern Virginia Review: "Istanbul," "On the Anniversary of Your Disappearance"

Folio: "In Therapy I Painted a Piñata Doll"

Fourteen Hills: "Mortuary Band on Stockton Street," "Powell Street"

Poet Lore: "Through the Stockton Street Tunnel"

Switchback: "The Green Umbrella"

Verdad: "Letter to Emily Dickinson"

"As He Lay Dying" received a first place poetry prize from *Calliope;* "On the Anniversary of Your Disappearance" received the Northern Virginia Poetry Prize.

I am forever grateful to Meg Day for selecting this manuscript, to the publisher Headmistress Press: Mary Meriam, Risa Denenberg, and Rita Mae Reese, to Mary Meriam for all her work in designing this book.

Many thanks to my teachers and readers at the Jenny McKean Moore Workshop, Northern Virginia Community College, George Mason University, Breadloaf Writers' Conference, Sewanee Conference, and elsewhere.

My deepest respect and gratitude to Jen Daniels, Sally Keith, Bruce Snider, Jennifer Atkinson, Jan Starkey, Susan Tichy, Alicia Stallings, John Patterson, Ana Delgadillo, Bill Neumire, Donald Illich, and Steve Mueske.

Love to Cassandra and Carlotta, my family, and friends.

About the Author

Carina Yun is a poet, artist, and a public servant living in Northern Virginia. She received her Masters of Science degree in 2008, and is currently pursuing an MFA in Poetry. Her poems have made appearances at *Adrienne; Beltway Poetry Quarterly; CutBank; The Feminist Wire; The Northern Virginia Review; Poet Lore;* and elsewhere. She is the winner of the Northern Virginia Review Poetry Prize and the Charlotte Mew Chapbook Prize in 2015. Her interests include law, poetry, visual art, languages (French & Mandarin), queer theory, traveling, and cycling. *On Loving a Saudi Girl* is her first collection of poems.

Headmistress Press Books

Lovely - Lesléa Newman
Teeth & Teeth - Robin Reagler
How Distant the City - Freesia McKee
Shopgirls - Marissa Higgins
Riddle - Diane Fortney
When She Woke She Was an Open Field - Hilary Brown
God With Us - Amy Lauren
A Crown of Violets - Renée Vivien tr. Samantha Pious
Fireworks in the Graveyard - Joy Ladin
Social Dance - Carolyn Boll
The Force of Gratitude - Janice Gould
Spine - Sarah Caulfield
Diatribe from the Library - Farrell Greenwald Brenner
Blind Girl Grunt - Constance Merritt
Acid and Tender - Jen Rouse
Beautiful Machinery - Wendy DeGroat
Odd Mercy - Gail Thomas
The Great Scissor Hunt - Jessica K. Hylton
A Bracelet of Honeybees - Lynn Strongin
Whirlwind @ Lesbos - Risa Denenberg
The Body's Alphabet - Ann Tweedy
First name Barbie last name Doll - Maureen Bocka
Heaven to Me - Abe Louise Young
Sticky - Carter Steinmann
Tiger Laughs When You Push - Ruth Lehrer
Night Ringing - Laura Foley
Paper Cranes - Dinah Dietrich
On Loving a Saudi Girl - Carina Yun
The Burn Poems - Lynn Strongin
I Carry My Mother - Lesléa Newman
Distant Music - Joan Annsfire
The Awful Suicidal Swans - Flower Conroy
Joy Street - Laura Foley
Chiaroscuro Kisses - G.L. Morrison
The Lillian Trilogy - Mary Meriam
Lady of the Moon - Amy Lowell, Lillian Faderman, Mary Meriam
Irresistible Sonnets - ed. Mary Meriam
Lavender Review - ed. Mary Meriam

www.ingramcontent.com/pod-product-compliance
Lightning Source LLC
Chambersburg PA
CBHW070040070426
42449CB00012BA/3113